Larry Lizard & Friends
60 Colouring
Images for Kids

Copywrite2021
John Wogan

Hi There _______________ I am delighted that you are now one of my Friends.
We are going to have so much fun together.
My other friends are inside this book
One picture per page and
with backgrounds. You will have hours of fun colouring each page.
But please remember to give each a new name.
Then they will be your friends too.
Your Friend
Larry Lizard

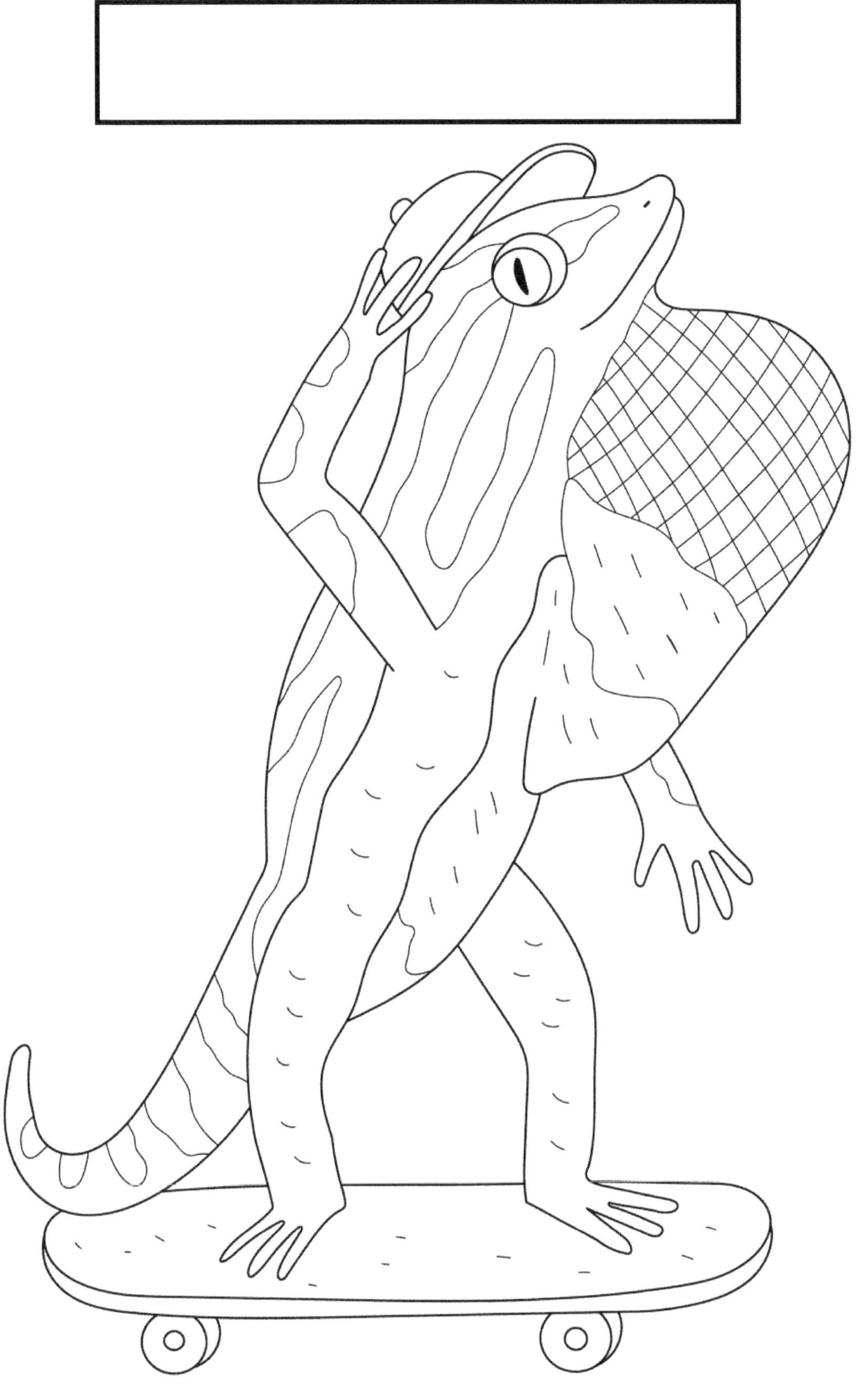

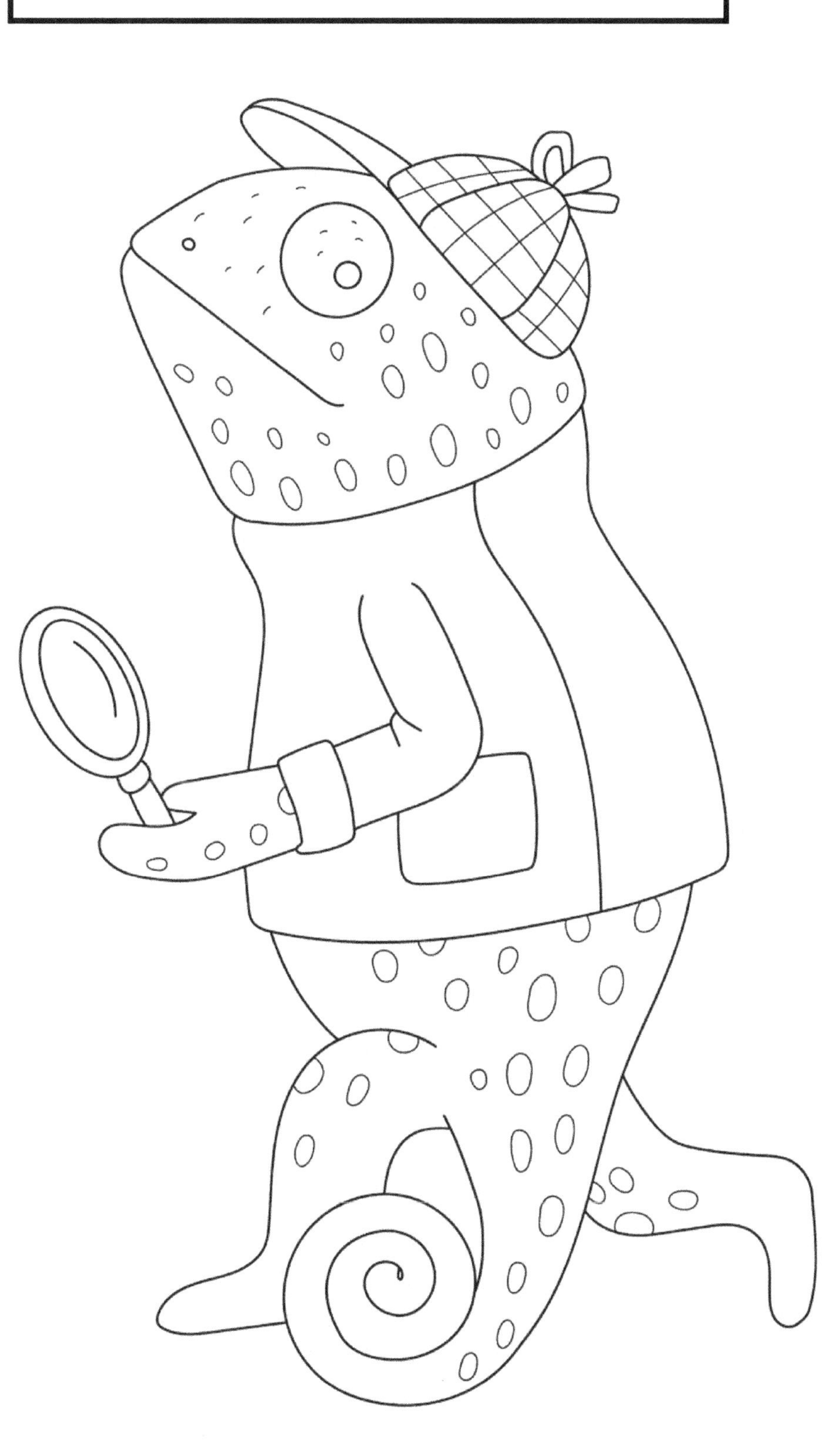

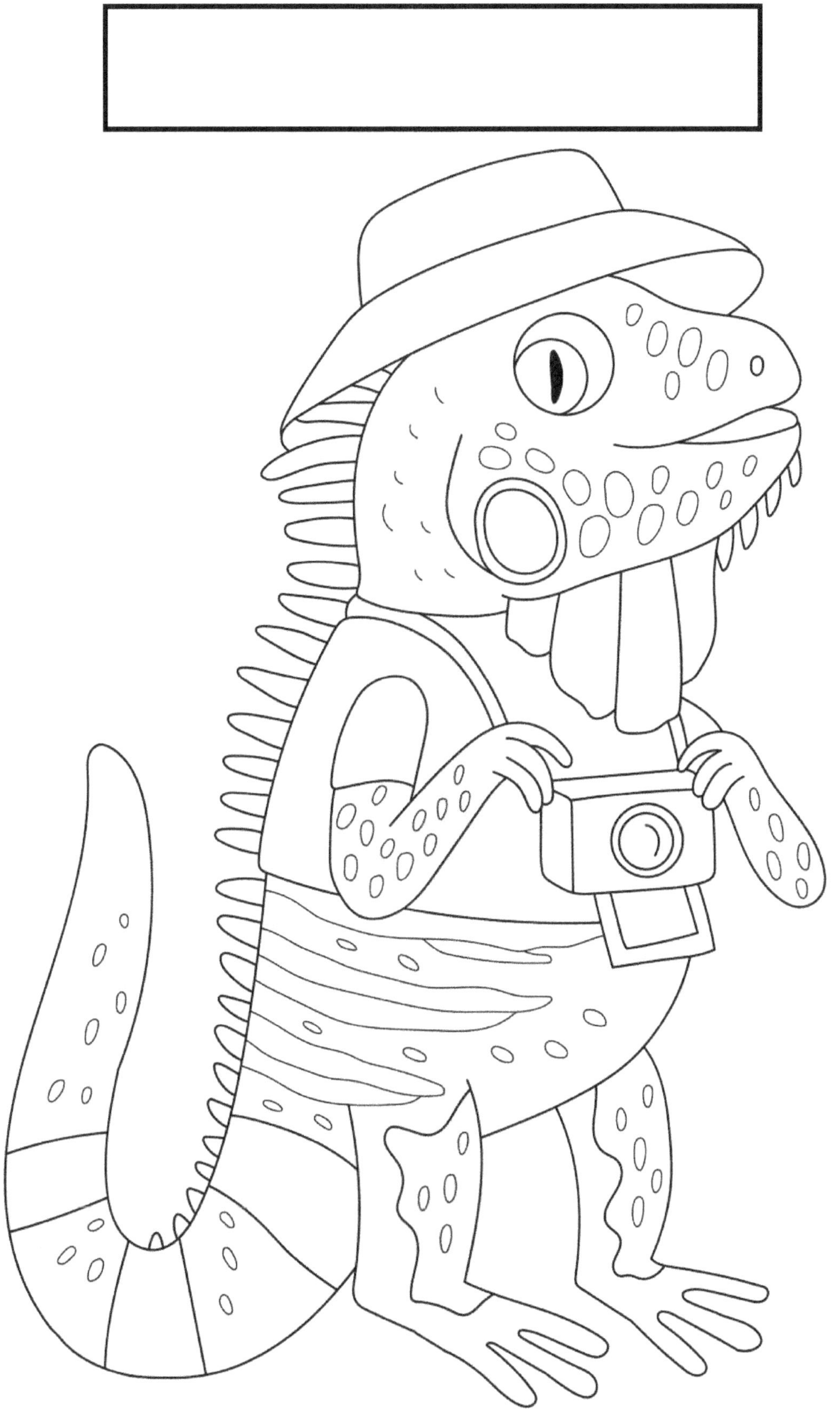

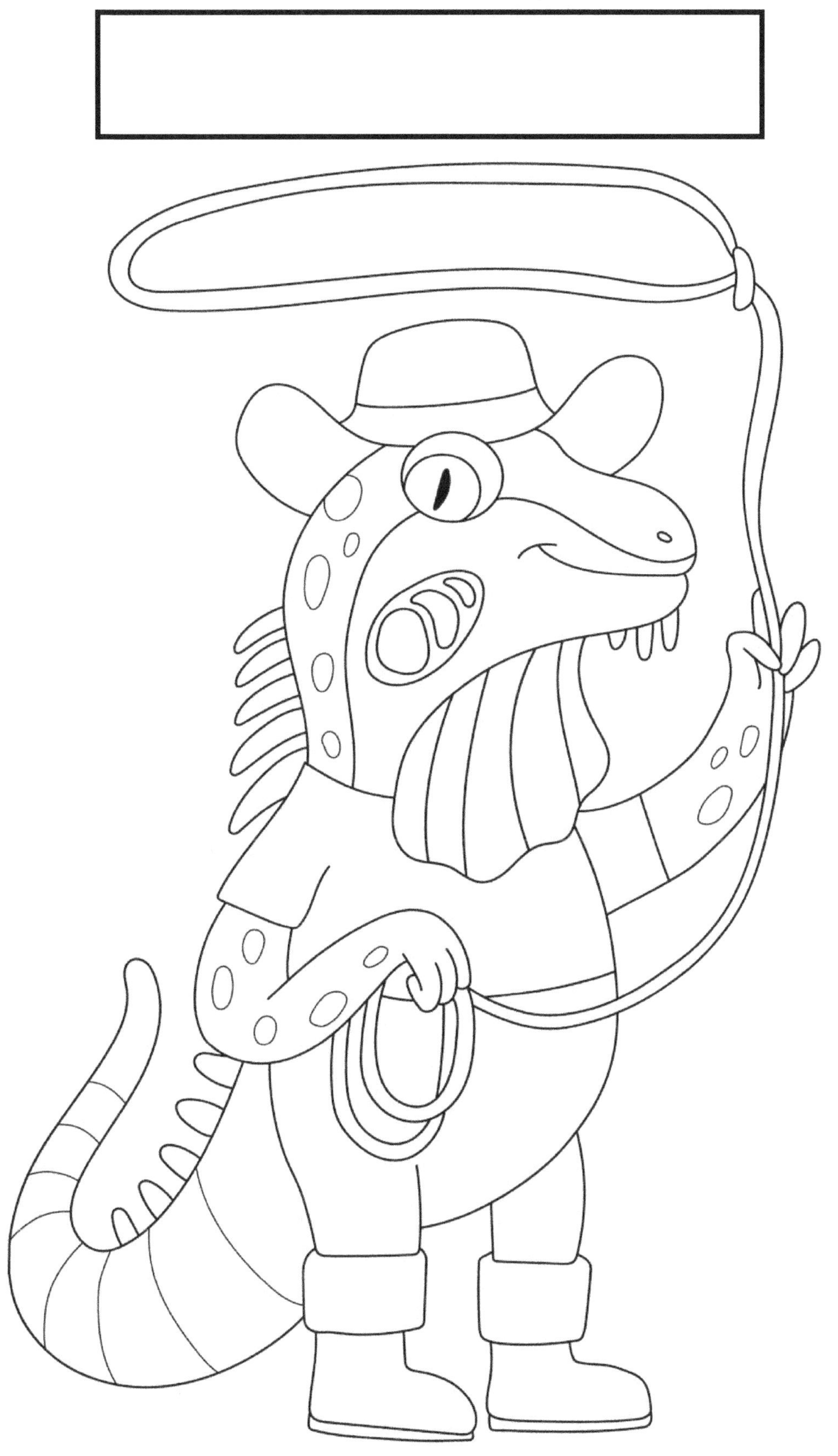

Hope you enjoy
Larry Lizard & Friends
Colouring Book.

If you want more quality
Colouring Books and Journals
Please head over to my Author
Page
Here on Amazon
Or go to website
https://jwbookstore.com